The Univers... TRIVIA BOOK

by
Jessica Lacher-Feldman

Hill Street Press  Athens, Georgia

A HILL STREET PRESS BOOK

Published in the United States of America by
Hill Street Press LLC
191 East Broad Street, Suite 216 • Athens, Georgia 30601-2848 USA
706-613-7200
info@hillstreetpress.com • www.hillstreetpress.com

Hill Street Press is committed to preserving the written word. Every effort is made to
print books on acid-free paper with a significant amount of post-consumer recycled
content. • Hill Street Press books are available in bulk purchase and customized
editions to institutions and corporate accounts. Please contact us for more information.
• No material in this book may be reproduced, scanned, stored, or transmitted in any
form, including all electronic and print media, or otherwise used without the prior
written consent of the publisher. However, an excerpt not to exceed twenty entries
may be used one time only by newspaper and magazine editors solely in conjunction
with a review of or feature article about this book, the authors, or Hill Street Press, LLC.
Attribution must be provided including the publisher's name, author's name, and title
of the book.

Text and cover design by Anne Richmond Boston.

Composition by Jenifer Carter

Printed in the United States of America.

Library of Congress Cataloging-in-Publication Data

Lacher-Feldman, Jessica.
    University of Alabama trivia book / by Jessica Lacher-Feldman.
         p.   cm.
    Includes bibliographical references.
    ISBN-13: 978-1-58818-116-9 (alk. paper)
    ISBN-10: 1-58818-116-2 (alk. paper)
  1. University of Alabama--Miscellanea. I. Title.
  LD71.8.L33 2006   378.761'84--dc22   2006017073

ISBN # 1-58818-116-2
10 9 8 7 6 5 4 3 2 1

First printing

Contents

The *University of Alabama Trivia Book* contains a ton of information—some of it is frivolous, some of it is serious, but all of it true!

Through these snippets of information, one can glean a great deal of information about this beloved institution—the capstone of higher education in Alabama. From its founding in 1831, The University of Alabamaa has seen a great amount of history. From the burning of the campus by Federal troops in 1865, to that day in June 1963 when all the world was focused on Foster Auditorium when Vivian Malone and James Hood walked through those doors to register for classes—and the days and years before, between and after, The University of Alabamaa has been a center of life for countless men, women and children.

The trivia questions and quotations in this book focus on many aspects of life at The University of Alabamaa. Chapters on student life and traditions, alumni, faculty, administrative leaders, campus and of course sports, will provide the reader with hours of entertainment, providing mind-bending facts on the triumphant, the brilliant, the funny and the bizarre.

Trivia isn't trivial. The little snippets of information gathered here, along with quotes from some of the best known and even relatively unknown people who have been associated with The University of Alabamaa represent a broad cross-section of life at UA, past, present and future. As a relative newcomer to Alabama, and to The University of Alabamaa, (and yes, a Yankee), I had my work cut out for me. But as an archivist working with materials relating to the history and culture of this fine university, I was primed for such a task. Trivia is even less trivial for me—as I spent hours looking through campus newspapers, yearbooks, manuscript collections and other published materials, I found out so much more about the university: obscure facts, forgotten lore and exciting tidbits that will help me make my job more interesting, and in turn, create future programs and exhibits in special collections that will be of interest to the university community and beyond.

This volume is not meant to represent everything there is to know about The University of Alabamaa, but rather it gives those interested parties, whether they are current students, alumni, fans or anyone else, some insight into the university's history and direction through the questions and quotes presented here.

I'd like to thank several people for their insight, creativity, suggestions and support. They include—but are not limited to—Thomas Little, Astro, Merrily Harris, Joyce Lamont, Jennifer Mathews, Erika Pribanic-Smith, Joanna Jacobs, Steve Gillis and everyone at the W.S. Hoole Special Collections Library, and to those whose works on The University of Alabamaa and Tuscaloosa have helped me so much, especially Suzanne Wolfe, Guy Hubbs, Robert Mellown and the late James Sellers. I'd also like to thank the countless thousands of people whose lives were touched by UA. I hope that you will enjoy looking through this and stumping your friends with obscure facts as much as I enjoyed putting this together and testing anyone who would listen. Roll Tide!

"In Alabama, you better be for football or you might as well leave."

—Bear Bryant

Student Life and Tradition

What is *Rammer Jammer?*

The now-defunct University of Alabama humor magazine that was published from the 1920s through the 1960s.

What is the "yellow hammer"?

The Alabama state bird.

What policy regarding "Rammer Jammer, Yellow Hammer!" was put in place in 2003?

The athletics department ruled that the Million Dollar Band could not play the cheer during games. The band is now allowed to play the cheer only once, after a victory.

What temporary setback did the cheer have in 1987 and 1994?

The Million Dollar Band was banned from playing "Rammer Jammer, Yellow Hammer!" by then-Athletic Director Steve Sloan because of the word "hell" in the cheer. The ban lasted until September 1989. In 1994 the athletics department again banned the cheer, this time in response to a request by the NCAA to minimize taunting and fighting at football games. In 1996 the cheer was reinstated. The band is now allowed to play the cheer only once, after a victory.

What is the name of The University of Alabama fight song?

"Yea Alabama."

Who wrote "Yea Alabama"?

Then-UA student and editor of the *Crimson White*, Ethelred "Lundy" Sykes. It was a response to a contest sponsored by *Rammer Jammer* magazine.

What is the *Corolla*? When was it first published? Who was its first editor-in-chief?

The University of Alabama's yearbook. 1893. Thomas Atkins Street Jr.

Name the two student-published literary journals at The University of Alabama.

The Black Warrior Review and *Marr's Field Journal.* *BWR* is the graduate publication, *Marr's,* the undergraduate.

Who was the first editor of the *Black Warrior Review*?

Jeannie Thompson, 1974.

What is "Hilaritas"?

A celebration of holiday music performed on campus annually since 1969.

Who was the first African-American student to become a member of the UA debate team?

Delores Boyd, who went on to practice law and is now a judge in Alabama.

How much did it cost to attend The University of Alabama in the early 1870s?

$130 per semester (term), which included tuition, board, fuel, lights, attendance and incidentals.

Who was the first African-American student to be admitted to The University of Alabama?

Autherine Lucy, in 1956.

What was the Cotillion Club? Where did these programs take place?

A club that organized dances, balls and other functions on campus. In the era of the big band, they brought such famous dance bands to campus, such has Harry James and His Music Makers, Tommy Dorsey, Les Brown, Benny Goodman and Spike Jones. Foster Auditorium, which remains best known for Wallace's "Stand."

What year were the Blackfriars founded?

1906.

What were the Corolla Beauties?

They were female UA students, who were selected each year to be featured in full page photographs in the yearbook.

Who chose the Corolla Beauties for 1949?

Billy Rose, legendary Broadway producer and lyricist. Other judges through the years included Rock Hudson, Pat Boone, Jackie Gleason, and UA football hero and Hollywood cowboy Johnny Mack Brown.

How many Greek associations, fraternities and sororities are recognized on the UA campus today?

Forty-eight.

Who are the McNair Scholars?

An elite group of students who, as juniors and seniors, work with faculty mentors and conduct research. The program is named for Dr. Ronald E. McNair, an astronaut who died in the Challenger space shuttle accident in January 1986.

Why were the stairs at what is now known as Reese-Phiefer Hall seldom used?

A campus legend said that only women of dubious virtue dared climb the stairs—probably due to the combination of wind and skirts on the massive staircase. This legend persisted until the 1970s when dress codes for women were abandoned.

What is "Mark's Madness"?

UA's student organization of basketball fans—named in honor of Coach Mark Gottfried.

What long-gone local student hangout was known for "good things to eat"?

Pug's cafeteria.

What exciting new feature did Pug's offer UA students in the fall 1955 semester?

Access to their new "TV Room"—which featured a rare color television for students to enjoy.

In one of her regular National Public Radio commentaries, UA English professor Diane Roberts described walking by an on-campus fraternity house and seeing its front yard occupied by a live goat and a bathtub containing a sleeping young woman in full evening dress. Which frat house was it?

The DKE house.

In what year did the BAMA Radio Network begin broadcasting?

1942. It evolved into WABP, the first student radio station at UA.

What unlikely pair roomed together at UA in the spring 1942 semester?

George Wallace and "Shorty" Price.

"The University is a well-spring of opportunity. All it takes for students to become active in University life is willingness to give a little bit of their time. The awards will come...."

—Ed Howard, 1984-5 editor of the Crimson White

When was the first televised pep rally in the history of The University of Alabama?

November 22, 1955, televised on WBIQ Channel 10 in Birmingham and WTIQ Channel 7 on Mt. Cheaha, (the highest point in the state).

Who was Alabama to play?

Auburn.

In 1956, how many date nights were freshman women allowed weekly?

Three: Friday, Saturday and one other night of their choice.

What was used as a shield in the 19th century in a duel to determine the University Steward?

According to a 1933 *Alumni News Magazine*, a side of bacon.

When women were first admitted to UA, what did they wear?

According to a letter from the president of the university in 1901, they were required to wear "a simple black uniform consisting of Oxford cap and gown, in all public places, especially when attending your classes."

In what year did individual photographs of undergraduate students first appear in the *Corolla?*

1913.

What senior honor society for men was founded by the class of 1914 and still continues its practice of tapping new members annually on the first Tuesday of May?

The Jasons

What change did the Jasons undergo in 1976?

They were officially banned from campus by UA administration for not admitting women.

Which student made national news in 2000 when she attempted to integrate UA's Greek system?

Melody Twilley. She went on to help found the Alpha Delta Sigma multicultural sorority in 2003.

What UA freshman successfully integrated the traditionally white sorority system in 2003?

Carla Ferguson, a freshman from Tuscaloosa. She was offered a bid by Gamma Phi Beta sorority.

What was "Guidon"? Who were among its first members?

A military fraternity for women. A chapter was established at UA in 1935. Margaret Denny, the daughter of then-President Denny, and Mary Harmon Black, the future Mrs. Paul "Bear" Bryant.

What is "Get on Board Day?"

The annual campus-wide extra-curricular activities fair, held on the Quad.

Who was the first SGA president? Who was he named for?

Lister Hill, who went on to be a US Senator. His father named him for Dr. Joseph Lister, under whom he studied. Dr. Lister was the pioneer of antiseptic surgery and the namesake of Listerine!

When was the SGA officially formed?

In 1914, though its initial formation as an organization for students to govern themselves began in 1907.

What year did the famed UA humor magazine *Rammer Jammer* cease publication? What publication replaced it?

In 1956, after thirty-one years. The *Mahout.*

What is a "mahout"?

A Hindu word meaning the keeper and driver of an elephant.

Where did the name "Million Dollar Band" come from?

The name "Million Dollar Band" is purported to have been bestowed in 1922 by W.C. "Champ" Pickens, an Alabama alumnus.

Besides pumping up Tide fans and players at games, what did the Million Dollar Band do in January of 1949?

Participated in US President Harry Truman's inauguration in Washington DC.

Where did UA's colors come from?

They were adopted after their use in the 1885 New Orleans Exposition competitive drill by UA's cadet class Company E, which won first place.

What legend is associated with the Denny Chimes?

Passed down by students, it is said that bricks will fall from the monument on the head of any virgin who walks too close to the chimes.

What prestigious honorary society was first established at UA in November of 1850 in secret?

Phi Beta Kappa

What was the first student society established at UA with the mission of the "promotion of literature and science"?

The Erosophic Society, in May of 1831.

What were the mottos of the Erosophic Society and Philomathic Society, respectively?

Erosophic Society: *Sapientia Praestat Omnibus*—Wisdom Precedes All Philomathic Society: *Pro Virtute et Patria*—For Valor and Country

What is Derby Day?

A spring celebration and competition between sororities at UA.

What is "pomping"?

The act of making elaborate and brightly colored signs with chicken wire and tissue paper for UA's homecoming weekend.

Where are these signs displayed?

On Sorority Row.

What fraternity continues to host the popular spring contest that once featured elaborate skits performed by various sororities and even the crowning of a queen of the derby?

Sigma Chi.

In October 1941, a dance was held on campus to collect what for G.I.s?

Cigarettes!

What happened to the *Crimson White* in 1942?

The editions were made physically smaller because of a wartime effort to conserve paper and a lack of advertising.

Oldest women's organization on campus?

The YWCA, which established a branch on campus in 1899.

What was the "Alabama Belle"? What was her fate?

The University of Alabama's replica 19th-century showboat. After only a few short months on the water in 1974, she sank in the Black Warrior River, was raised by divers, but then sank again—permanently.

Who was the first African-American homecoming queen?

Terry Points, in 1973.

Who were the "Alabama Cavaliers"?

A college band at UA—and one of the largest in the South. They formed in 1929 and played through the 1950s.

What was *The Bama Beam*?

The University of Alabama's engineering magazine.

What UA student organization founded in 1997 brings a little-known sport to T-Town?

The Crimson Cricket Club. The club is made up largely of UA students from India.

What is the Mallet Assembly and where do they live?

A self-governing men's residential honorary, founded in 1961. Counter to its name and definition, the Mallet Assembly does admit women, and not all Malleteers, (as they're called), live in Byrd Hall.

What student organization, which celebrates its 35th anniversary in 2006, has recorded two full-length albums?

The Afro-American Gospel Choir, founded in 1971.

The soundtrack to which mid-1970s off-Broadway musical was a favorite for the DJs at WVUA during the 1980s?

Tuscaloosa's Calling Me, but I'm Not Going, by Hank Beebe, Bill Heyer and Sam Dann.

Faculty

What current UA history professor won the prestigious Lincoln Prize in 2003 for his book *Frederickburg! Fredericksburg!* (UNC Press, 2003).

Dr. George Rable.

What current UA English professor is known for discovering a previously unknown poem by William Shakespeare?

Dr. Gary Taylor, who discovered the poem, "Shall I Die? Shall I Fly?" in 1985.

"My total experience as a student at this great institution was rewarding and long-lasting. Friendships made there have enriched my life and become more meaningful…."

—Woodrow W. Clements, former UA student (1933-35)

What former UA professor designed the long-used red, white and blue crest used as the emblem of the Ford Motor Company?

Art professor Frank Engle. He taught at UA from 1949 until 1980.

What former University professor went on to have a college named in his honor? What Northern college is named in his honor?

F.A.P. Barnard, an antebellum UA professor of astronomy. He was the first professor hired for the UA College of Engineering. Barnard College. He taught for many years at Columbia College (now Columbia University). Barnard is a women's college affiliated with Columbia.

Who left The University of Alabamaa in 1837 and opened the noted antebellum Greene School for Boys ten years later?

Henry Tutwiler.

What did prize-winning novelist Russell Banks (author of *The Sweet Hereafter* and *Cloudsplitter*) take back home with him after his time as a visiting professor in the UA English department?

A wife. While in Tuscaloosa in 1987, Banks met Chase Twichell, a professor in the MFA program, and they were married in 1989.

What former UA history professor served as the longtime editor of *The Alabama Review* and has done extensive research and writing on the Gorgas family?

Dr. Sarah Woolfolk Wiggins.

What current UA faculty member was awarded the prestigious Carnegie National Outstanding Doctoral and Research Universities Professor of the Year in 2001?

Professor Cornelius Carter, of UA's Department of Theater and Dance.

What soon-to-be bestselling author left his job as a professor at UA under a cloud of mystery in 1927?

Carl Carmer, author of *Stars Fell on Alabama.*

What art professor emeritus never completed more than a high school degree?

Al Sella

What former UA professor held the Coal Royalty Chairholder in Poetry at UA in 1990?

George Starbuck.

Two volumes of the poet's work, which were published posthumously, were co-edited by a UA professor. Who was it?

Dr. Elizabeth Meese.

Name the former UA faculty member who, wrote several Alabama history textbooks used in Alabama schools for decades.

Dr. Charles A. Summersell.

What current UA faculty member is one of the foremost experts on the relationship between Thomas Jefferson and Sally Hemming?

Dr. Joshua D. Rothman. His publications include the 2004 article "Hardly Sallygate: Thomas Jefferson, Sally Hemings, and the Sex Scandal That Wasn't."

What former UA professor published a book on her great-grandmother, the "official White House hostess" who took over for an ailing First Lady?

Elizabeth Tyler Coleman, who taught English at UA, wrote a biography of Priscilla Cooper Tyler, who served as the official White House hostess for her father-in-law, President John Tyler, after his wife suffered a stroke. *Priscilla Cooper Tyler and the American Scene 1816-1889* was published in 1955.

What UA professor of geology was appointed to be the first state geologist in Alabama?

Professor Michael Tuomey. He was appointed in 1848 and served until his death in 1857.

What "military man" brought the Million Dollar Band into national prominence? Where did the Colonel get his rank?

Colonel Carleton K. Butler, who led the band from 1935 to 1968. It was conferred upon him by the University's ROTC in 1938.

What former UA faculty member founded and directed a world-renowned string quartet at UA? What did his students call him?

Professor Ottokar Cadek. Professor Cadek joined the faculty in 1943 and headed violin instruction and chamber music until his death in 1956. "Papa."

What UA professor served as a consultant for Stephen Spielberg's film _Amistad_?

Dr. Howard Jones. A professor of history at UA since 1974, his book _Mutiny on the Amistad_ received wide critical acclaim.

Name the author who both graduated from and taught at UA who penned an important work that he did not live to see published.

Clarence Cason, a 1917 graduate and author of _Ninety Degrees in the Shade_. His life ended tragically just days before the book was released.

What former faculty member and UA graduate received the Palmes Academique from the French government in the 1950s?

Professor Wade H. Coleman.

Which famous novelist and short story writer published an essay in *The New Yorker* recalling his experience of being robbed at gunpoint in front of a downtown Tuscaloosa bar during his time as a visiting English professor? Which bar was it?

Andre Dubus, author of *In the Bedroom*. The Chukker

Name the former UA professor who gained international notoriety in 1997 by leading a mass suicide.

Leader of the Heaven's Gate cult, Marshall Applewhite. Known as "Do," in reference to the musical notation, he taught organ at UA in the late '50s.

What former UA art professor made models of original campus buildings for UA's 125th anniversary in 1956?

Howard Goodson.

Who was the first woman on the UA faculty?

Amelia Gayle Gorgas, who stepped in as University librarian upon the death of her husband, Josiah.

What former UA professor served as president of Sweet Briar College for twenty years? On what Alabama native did she author a biography published by The University of Alabama Press?

Dr. Anne Gary Pannell; the youngest woman ever to earn a doctoral degree at Oxford University. She wrote the 1961 biography *Julia S. Tutwiler and Social Progress in Alabama.*

"With the mellow tones of Denny Chimes in the background I found, through the challenge of outstanding professors... that studying and learning are exciting experiences."

—Frank Minis Johnson Jr., 1943 UA Law School graduate

What former UA dean, faculty member and alum helped organize the Oak Ridge Nuclear Studies Institute?

Dr. Eric Rodgers. He received his bachelor's and master's degrees from UA in 1931 and 1932 and taught in the physics department for almost forty years.

What campus building is named in his honor?

Eric and Sarah Rodgers Library for Science and Engineering is named for Professor Rodgers and his wife.

What did Sarah Rodgers do at UA?

Professor Sarah Rodgers taught statistics in the College of Commerce and Business Administration for more than forty years. She received her bachelor's degree from UA.

What former UA professor has work in well over a dozen major museum's permanent collections?

Professor Richard Zoellner. Professor Zoellner taught art at UA from 1945 until 1979 and remained active with campus life and exhibited work until his death in 2003 at the age of 94.

What program did Professor Zoellner create on campus?

Zoellner established one of only two departments of fine art printmaking in the Southeast at UA in 1945.

Which former UA professor was knighted by the King of Sweden? On whom did he write a critically acclaimed biography?

Hudson Strode, professor of creative writing.
Jefferson Davis.

What former UA professor wrote a definitive work on Walter Lippmann and freedom of the press?

Professor John Luskin, who taught at UA from 1938 until 1974.

What UA professor spearheaded an effort in 2005 to produce "Memories: Perspectives of Black History," to document the voices and stories of the people who were involved in the tumultuous days of the struggle for civil rights in Tuscaloosa.

Dr. Jerry Rosenberg, professor of psychology and director of UA's New College Radio Lab.

What former faculty member was the recipient of the first Kennedy Center-Rockefeller Foundation International Piano Competition in 1978?

Professor Bradford Gowen of the music department. He received a standing ovation following his performance at the Kennedy Center.

What UA English professor is internationally recognized as an expert on authors and the experience of war?

UA English professor Dr. Philip Beidler. Dr. Beilder has also authored and edited three books on Alabama authors.

What UA professor established the debate team on campus?

Annabell Dunham Hagood. The team won national championships under her guidance in 1949 and in 1955.

How many instructors were in the nursing college when it was first established at UA?

Just one—the program built from there, and moved to Birmingham in 1967. The Capstone College of Nursing at UA opened in 1976 and currently has more than forty faculty and adjunct instructors.

What current UA professor is an internationally known scholar of Jacques Derrida, having translated three of his major works?

Dr. Richard Rand in UA's Department of English. Dr. Rand has also edited two works on this French philosopher.

What UA professor helped establish two museums relating to African-American heritage in Alabama?

Dr. Amilcar Shabazz.

What former UA professor and alum penned the novels *From Hell to Breakfast, Night Fire*, and *The Secret Pilgrim?*

> Ed Kimbrough, who received degrees at UA in 1939 and 1940, and taught in the creative writing program from 1941 until his death in 1965.

What former UA professor was the first graduate of UA's Radio Arts program?

> Roy Flynn, who joined the faculty in 1944. Flynn was also a published fiction writer.

What former UA professor recorded more than 500 songs, including lullabies, African-American gospel and secular songs, temperance songs and work songs in the 1940s?

> Byron Arnold, former professor in the Department of Music.

What current UA professor and dean spent two decades working with Arnold's material and published *An Alabama Songbook* in 2004?

> Dr. Robert Halli, professor of English and dean of the Honors College.

What former UA history professor contributed to the monumental work, *I'll Take My Stand: The South and the Agrarian Tradition*, published by Harper Brothers in 1930?

Frank Owsley. His essay is entitled "The Irrepressible Conflict".

What UA professor emeritus is one of the most prolific and influential scholars of early America, the Founding Fathers, and federalism, and penned a definitive biography on Alexander Hamilton?

Dr. Forrest McDonald of UA's history department.

What unusual sartorial study habit did Dr. McDonald admit to on a C-SPAN book program that was aired on national television?

When home alone, he prefers to work in the nude.

"My memory teems with pictures of thousands of students with amazing variety of careers on campus and after graduate. I taught at least one bishop-to-be, artists, actors, novelists, and so many others that the list would quickly get out of hand. Academic friendship is a tremendously important element in education (I think in these days underrated. The University of Alabama has enriched my life with generations of friend—mentors, fellow students, colleagues, and my own students. I am grateful."

—George Burke Johnston, UA graduate and former UA Professor and assistant dean

Alumni

Who was the only UA alum to have won two Pulitzer Prizes?

E.O. Wilson (classes of 1949, 1950), both in the non-fiction category. He won in 1979 for his book *On Human Nature* and in 1991 for his book *The Ants.*

What UA cheerleader and homecoming queen went on to win two Emmy Awards and a Golden Globe, in addition to penning a *New York Times* bestseller?

Sela Ward (class of 1977).

What UA alum, known for his stereotypical Southern drawl, has a star on the Hollywood Walk of Fame? What character was he best known for?

Jim Nabors (class of 1952). Gomer Pyle on the *Andy Griffith Show,* and the successful spin-off, *Gomer Pyle, U.S.M.C.*

In what other area of entertainment has Jim Nabors excelled?

Music—he has recorded well over thirty albums, earning three gold records.

What far-out psychologist enrolled at The University of Alabama in the 1941?

Timothy Leary. He was expelled for spending the night in a women's dormitory, losing his student deferment, and was drafted into military service in 1943. He then took college courses at night and earned a BS from The University of Alabama that same year.

What UA alum sold more books than any other American author between the two world wars?

T.S. Stribling—he even outsold his leading contemporaries, Faulkner and Hemingway, and is considered by many the leader of the Southern Literary Renaissance.

What Tuscaloosa native and UA graduate is considered one of the most important physicists of the 20th century? What were his three older brothers known for?

> Robert Jemison Van de Graff, inventor of the Van de Graff generator. Football! Adrian (class of 1912), Hargrove (class of 1914) and William T. "Bully" (class of 1915) Van de Graff all played for the Crimson Tide.

What 1906 UA Law School grad served on the US Supreme Court?

> Hugo L. Black (1886-1971).

What UA alum went on to produce such films as *Die Hard* and *Field of Dreams*?

> Charles (Chuck) Gordon, a former ZBT at UA.

Name the two well-known cousins who both are in UA's C&IS Hall of Fame.

> Mel Allen and Elmo Ellis—both giants in the world of broadcasting.

What other hallowed halls does Mel Allen grace?

He has been honored by the National Radio Hall of Fame, the Baseball Hall of Fame and the Alabama Sports Hall of Fame.

What honors has Elmo Ellis earned? What distinction did Elmo Ellis have while a student at UA?

Too many to list—but among them a 1966 Peabody Award and UA's highest individual accolade, the Hugo Black Award, in 2000. He is the only student to ever serve as editor of three main UA student publications—the *Crimson White*, the *Corolla*, and the now-defunct humor magazine, *Rammer Jammer.*

What UA alum and famous composer's nephew went on to invent the tele-prompter, revolutionizing live television?

Irving Berlin Kahn, class of 1939.

What UA alum earned three degrees in seven years—a record pace.

Mike Stevenson: He began his study at UA in 1994, and by 2001, he had received his bachelor's, master's and doctoral degrees in metallurgical and materials engineering.

What well-known fiction writer graduated from UA in 1949?

Borden Deal, author of several novels, including *Walk through the Valley*.

Before penning his first of many novels, what did prize-winning author William Bradford Huie do after graduation from the UA in 1930?

He lived in Tiflis, in the then-Soviet Union, and returned to the US to lecture and write on Russian life, writing for such magazines as the *National Republic*.

What two Alabama governors served as SGA Presidents?

George Wallace (1942) and Don Siegelman (1967).

What MFA in creative writing graduate has authored several novels and has had one of her works adapted into a film? Where did she find her source material for this work?

Nanci Kincaid. Her 1998 fiction novel, *Balls*, brilliantly captures the experience of living as a coach's wife. She was the spouse of college football coach Dick Tomey.

What former UA student was a well-known author and astute businessman, as well as a decorated war hero and established art collector?

William March Campbell, who wrote under the name William March. He was a WWI Navy Cross and Croix de Guerre recipient, wrote several novels and short stories, and was a VP for the Waterman Streamship Company.

Who was the first director of the Million Dollar Band?

Dr. Gustav Wittig, who led the band from 1913 to 17. From 1917 to 27, it was led by students.

What 1905 UA School of Law graduate was awarded a Pulitzer Prize in Letters in 1933?

T.S. Stribling, for *The Store*. Though not read often today, it was an instant bestseller when *Time* magazine called it "easily the most important US novel of the year."

Which graduate of The University of Alabama College of Communication and veteran of UA's NPR affiliate WUAL became the national host of *Weekend All Things Considered* in 2005?

Debbie Elliot.

What UA alum was *King for a Day* on January 11, 1957?

Dr. R.C. Partlow (1912) was featured via telephone on this popular early television program.

> "Sure I'd love to beat Notre Dame, don't get me wrong. But nothing matters more than beating that cow college on the other side of the state!"
>
> **—Bear Bryant**

What cum laude graduate of UA went on to serve as the first director of the first state archives in the United States?

Thomas McAdory Owen (1866-1920). He was the founding director of the Alabama Department of Archives and History in Montgomery, which was founded in 1901, making it the oldest state archives in the United States.

What Tony-winning actor and UA alum (MFA, Alabama Shakespeare Festival) has joked that he has "the worst name in show business"?

Norbert Leo Butz, winner of the 2005 Tony award for best actor in a musical for his role as Freddy in *Dirty Rotten Scoundrels.*

Name the UA alum who went on to serve as CEO of Texaco and as a director of the American Petroleum Institute.

John Key McKinley—he holds both a bachelor's and master's degree from UA.

What UA alum got his start on the silver screen with Buster Crabb?

Yancey Brame, also credited as Bruce Lane and Yancey Lane (AB, 1926; AM, 1928). He appeared in several small film roles in the 1930s and 1940s.

What UA alum wrote a book which was voted "the best novel of the century" as voted by librarians across the United States?

Harper Lee—her novel *To Kill a Mockingbird* won her a Pulitzer Prize and has been translated into over forty languages.

What recent phenomenon has *To Kill a Mockingbird* also dominated?

The "One Book" program, where an entire community reads the same book. *Mockingbird* has been chosen for this project twenty-five times.

What honor was Harper Lee given by the Peck family? What literary endeavors did Harper Lee take on as a UA student?

Gregory Peck's grandson is named Harper in her honor. Peck received the best actor Oscar in 1962 for his role as Atticus Finch. Ms. Lee was active in literary matters, such as serving as the editor of *Rammer Jammer*, the University's literary and humor magazine, and writing a column "Caustic Comment" for the University newspaper, the *Crimson White*.

What student, who transferred to UA from Transylvania University in 1831, became its first graduate, earning his AB at UA's first commencement in 1832?

John Augustine Nooe.

What UA alum and Tuscaloosa native currently holds a US Senate seat and chairs two Senate Committees?

Senator Richard Shelby.

"I didn't meet Dr. Denny until I registered for admission to the law school at Alabama....He asked me to walk over to his office with him for a talk. He talked about the law school and about his son, a recent graduate. He suggested that I study my classmates as well as my books, since he expected that school to produce the future leaders of this state....I soon found out that Dr. Denny was right --- the leadership which would guide this state was in the law school. The associations formed there have directly influenced my entire life. "

—George LeMaistre, UA Law School graduate (1933).

What 1941 alumna served as a member of the Woman's Auxiliary Ferry Squadron and ferried both B-24 and B-26 planes to airfield and ports during World War II?

Nancy Batson, class of 1941.

On what magazine was she a "cover girl"?

She appeared on the cover of *Air Force* magazine, complete with leather bomber jacket and parachute!

What UA alum was responsible for bringing Dr. Pepper to the masses, making it more than just a regional drink in Texas?

Woodrow Wilson (Foots) Clements, who was CEO of Dr. Pepper from 1974 to 1980. He was inducted into the Beverage World Hall of Fame in 1982.

What UA alum wrote a play that was turned into a 1958 film starring Anthony Quinn and Shirley Booth?

Lonnie Coleman (1942), whose play *Next of Kin* was made into the film *Hot Spell*.

What UA alum wrote for such television shows as *Laverne and Shirley* and played the role of the mad scientist in 1950s Chiquita Banana commercials?

Paul B. Brice, a 1950 UA graduate.

What former senator and congressman (not from Alabama!) graduated from The University of Alabama in 1921?

Senator Claude Pepper. Senator Pepper was active in public service from 1929 until his death in 1989.

What class of 1956 graduate and winner of the Frank Thomas Memorial Trophy and the Jim Moore Memorial Trophy went on to do some very big things in a very cold place?

Bart Starr—Former UA quarterback, who became a superstar with the Green Bay Packers.

What other UA alum also played and coached with the Packers?

Don Hutson, who retired from pro football with four all-time records.

Which UA graduate celebrated her wedding in the President's Mansion?

Lua Galalee Martin, daughter of Dr. Galalee, UA president, 1948-1953.

What UA alum penned mystery novels along with some important bibliographic work on Confederate Imprints and 19th-century maps?

Sara Elizabeth Mason (1932).

What UA graduate is credited for the discovery of aureomycin, an important antibiotic?

Dr. Benjamin Minge Duggar (1891).

What UA alum was known for a time as "the statehood senator"?

Hon. Ralph E. Moody, who was selected to the Territorial Senate for the then-Territory of Alaska. He went on to serve as Alaska's attorney general from 1960 to 1962.

What UA alum was best known as the father of the Blue and Gray football game?

Champ Pickens (1898).

What was Champ Picken's early role in Alabama football? What was the result of that telegram? What was the score of that game?

It was Champ who sent the telegram to the chair of the Tournament of Roses Committee in 1925 to draw his attention to UA's winning record. Two weeks later, Alabama had a bid to the bowl. Alabama beat Washington 20-19.

What UA alum won the 1976 US Open Championship and returned to UA to complete his degree in 2001?

Golf legend Jerry Pate.

What other member of the Pate family graduated that year?

> Jerry Pate's daughter Jennifer received her degree in Human Development and Family Studies the same day!

What UA alum served as the editor of the *Crimson White* while a student in 1963 and facilitated articles that documented the integration of The University of Alabama?

> Scott Henry (Hank) Black Jr.

Name the UA alum who helped pen the controversial novel, *The Body Politic*, with Lynne Cheney, Vice President Dick Cheney's wife? What other VPs has he been associated with?

> Vic Gold, a UA Law School grad. He was the press secretary for Spiro Agnew and a speech writer and advisor to then-Vice President George Bush under the Reagan administration.

What former *CW* sports editor had an early start creating the experimental and literary column titled "Sports Gay-zing"? Besides his brilliant journalistic career and several well-known books, what honor was bestowed upon him in 2004?

Gay Talese (class of 1953). His most famous piece, "Frank Sinatra Has a Cold" was labeled "The Greatest Story Ever Told" in *Esquire's* 70th-anniversary issue—calling it the very best article in *Esquire's* long history of excellent articles.

What UA alum was a campus leader in the early 1970s and was one of the first presidents of UA's Afro-American Association?

John Bivens.

What UA grad served as attorney general and governor of Alabama, and had a starring role in a 1955 film?

John M. Patterson. The film, *The Phenix City Story*, was a sensational film noir drama about the murder of Patterson's father and newly elected attorney general Albert Patterson.

"All he's ever talked about is how much he loves the University of Alabama. Now that I'm in school there, I understand why."

—Jessica Namath, UA student and daughter of legendary UA quarterback Joe Namath

What UA alum and former president of the Chicago Medical School was the recipient of a Horatio Alger Award?

Dr. John J. Sheinin. Dr. Sheinin came to Alabama from Russia as a teen with just $4 in his pocket.

Name the former editor of the *New York Times* who received his master's degree from UA in 1973?

Howell Raines.

What former UA alum played football with the Tide and professional baseball, and then after World War II made monumental strides in yet another sport? What was the name of his inspiring book, published in 1969?

Charley Boswell. After losing his sight in WWII, he went on to win 28 US and international blind golfing championships and served as an advocate for vision-impaired athletes and as an inspiration to countless others. *Now I See.*

What UA alum was the first African-American Bama Belle and a founding member of UA's Afro-American Association, now called African-American Association?

Diane Kirksey. She was also the first African-American member of the homecoming court.

Whose voice will always be remembered as "the Voice of the Crimson Tide"? Where was he seen weekly?

John Forney, whose play-by-play was heard by countless thousands for years. As co-host of weekly television shows with Alabama head coaches Paul "Bear" Bryant and Gene Stallings.

What UA alum was the first woman to serve on the executive committee of the American Accounting Association?

Dr. Catherine Miles, who received her MS and PhD from UA in the early 1950s.

What UA alum with a ferocious nickname is considered the father of modern amphibious warfare?

General Holland M. "Howling Mad" Smith, USMC who received his LLB from UA in 1903.

What UA alum, who served as president of one of the largest manufacturing corporations in the world, was once told by a professor that he'd never recommend a man for a business career who spent his time in college "picking a banjo"?

Knox Ide, who graduated from UA in 1923, made his way to New York in 1931 after graduating from Harvard Law School and maintained a successful law career in Anniston. He later served as president of American Home Products Corporation.

What UA alum has written award-winning children's books and served as an airplane mechanic in the Women's Army Corps in WWII?

Aileen Kilgore Henderson. Her first book for children, *Summer of the Bonepile Monster*, won the Milkweed Prize for Children's Literature in 1995 and the Alabama Library Association Award in 1996.

Who was the first woman to earn a law degree at UA?

Mable Yerby, who later became Mrs. James Lawson, received her LLB from UA in 1920.

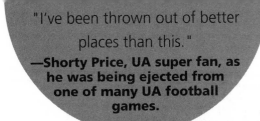

What famous Alabama brothers and UA graduates went on to Congress, with one serving in the US Senate and the other serving in the US House of Representatives? Among their other distinctions, what did they each do in turn?

Senator John H. Bankhead II and Congressman William Brockman Bankhead, respectively. Raised actress Tallulah Bankhead. After the death of her mother, William's daughter Tallulah was raised by her uncle John and his wife.

Who was the last surviving Confederate soldier who had been a UA student?

John Flournoy Ponder, who passed away in 1943 at the age of 95.

Who was the first African-American executive vice president of the SGA and a student representative to the UA Board of Trustees in 1975?

Sylvester Jones.

What UA alum has won three Emmy awards and a Peabody? With what two national heroes was he photographed as a student?

Chief Washington correspondent for *ABC News* and internationally recognized reporter, John Cochran, who received a BA from UA in 1963. President John F. Kennedy and Paul "Bear" Bryant. In the photo Cochran can be seen peeking over then-UA President Rose's shoulder.

Who gave John Cochran his first broadcasting job?

Another UA alum Burt Bank, now a fellow UA College of Communication and Information Sciences Hall of Famer. Bank hired Cochran when he was a student to announce records and read the news at WTBC radio in Tuscaloosa.

What did Burt Bank found in 1953? What horrific event has made Burt Bank's name widely known.

The University of Alabama Football Network. Major Burt Bank was a survivor of the infamous Bataan Death March.

Name the UA alum whose grandfather is credited with inventing the typewriter.

Gordon Sholes, whose great-grandfather Christopher Sholes patented his "type-writer" in 1868 and also developed the now-standard QWERTY keyboard configuration.

What UA alum helped found the CIA? What else was he known for? What legacy did he leave behind?

Miles Copeland Jr. (1937). He was an established jazz trumpet player and one of the first white musicians to play with an all-black orchestra. He played with Erskine Hawkins as well as other bands, most notably the Glenn Miller Orchestra. Besides his diplomatic work and publishing, his three sons, Miles III, Stewart and Ian, all have had incredibly successful music careers: Stewart was the drummer of the band The Police, Miles was the founder of IRS Records and Ian was a major concert promoter and booking agent.

"I just wanted to thank God for giving me the opportunity to coach at my alma mater and be part of the UA tradition."
—**Bear Bryant**

Who was the first African-American student to earn a PhD from UA?

Dr. Joffre T. Whisenton, in 1966.

What former UA student was crowned Miss Universe in 1967?

Sylvia Louise Hitchcock.

What internationally recognized artist and photographer received two degrees from UA? Despite having lived in Washington DC for decades, from where does he draw much of his influence?

William Christenberry, who received a BFA in 1958 and an MA in 1959. From the Alabama Black Belt—he makes frequent trips home to Tuscaloosa and to Hale County, Alabama.

Which graduate of the Alabama Shakespeare festival's Professional Actor's Training Program (in cooperation with the Ua Department of Theatre and Dance) received the 2001 Emmy for Outstanding Guest Actor in a Drama Series for his portrayal of a demented serial killer on TV's *The Practice?* What was his first and most famous role on the New York stage?

Michael Emerson. He played Oscar Wilde in Moises Kaufman's play *Gross Indecency.*

According to the October 1943 UA *Alumni Magazine*, how many living alumni were in military service at that time?

There were approximately 6,000 people, or 25 percent of the alumni, in all theaters of war.

What UA alum was the first woman to ever serve as the State Department spokesperson? To what country did she serve as ambassador?

Margaret Tutwiler (1973). Morocco.

What UA alum was one of the first African-American graduates of the UA School of Law and was appointed to the UA Board of Trustees in 2004?

Hon. John England. Judge England is a former member of the Alabama Supreme Court.

What UA alum was the first female FBI agent to be sent on assignment outside the United States?

Lois Drolet (1938). She was ordered to Hawaii in 1943—before Hawaii gained statehood.

What UA alum has written four successful novels and six screenplays for television?

Robert Inman.

What UA alum made history on campus in June 1963, but did not remain long?

Dr. James Hood. Along with Vivian Malone, he was one of the first two African-American students to enroll at UA in 1963 during the "Stand in the School House Door." While he did not complete his undergraduate degree at UA, he returned to earn his doctorate in 1997.

What UA alum was prevented from attending in 1956, but returned to receive a master's degree from UA in 1991?

Autherine Lucy Foster. She received her degree at the same ceremony as her daughter, who earned a bachelor's degree in finance.

"The circular structure was to reflect enlightenment, a sign of a modern university, because as, the English universities used the church as their focal point. Both Universities, Alabama and Virginia, used their libraries, housed in the rotundas, as their focal points, which was a secular view at that time, separating education and religion."

—Dr. Robert Mellown, Professor of Art History on the Rotunda

What internationally known painter's work was selected by FDR to hang in the White House? What area on campus holds three of his paintings?

Kelly Fitzpatrick (1910). His works were also hung in Supreme Court Judge Hugo Black's office, as well as in the office of Senator John Bankhead. The W.S. Hoole Special Collections Library on the UA campus. The paintings are part of a series depicting industries in Alabama.

What UA alum is the first to be chosen as a US astronaut? In what unique way did he earn his degree? Where did he travel in March of 2001?

Serving as a lieutenant colonel in the US Air Force, James M. Kelly is the first UA graduate to be selected as an astronaut. He earned his master's degree in aerospace engineering in 1996 through the QUEST, or Quality University Extended Site Telecourses program. He piloted the space shuttle Discovery on a mission to the International Space Station.

What 1951 UA graduate had a hand in Saturn, Apollo, Sky Lab and the space shuttle programs, and holds a patent for Rod Peening—Process and Tool Improvement?

Vincent P. Caruso. He was named a Distinguished Fellow of the UA Department of Industrial Engineering in 2000.

What UA alum and friend of Paul "Bear" Bryant was a groundbreaking newspaper owner, a Pulitzer Prize winner and a civil rights champion?

Hazel Brannon Smith (1935).

What 1999 grad (MFA, creative writing) won the coveted Yale Series of Younger Poets Competition in 2000?

Maurice Manning, for his critically acclaimed collection of poems, *Lawrence Booth's Book of Visions.*

What UA alum's short story "Time's End" appeared in the *Best Short Stories of 1943* and had several stories appear in publications such as *American Mercury* and the *Saturday Evening Post*?

Robert P. Gibbons. Gibbons was one of many of Hudson Strode's successful students.

Name the UA alum who served as assistant surgeon general of the United States.

Dr. Ralph C. Williams, a 1910 UA graduate, was appointed to the post in 1943.

Who was the first woman to receive a BA from UA?

Rosa Lawhorn, in 1900.

What UA alum made headlines around the world and has become a symbol of success and triumph for generations to come? What honor was bestowed upon her in 2000?

Vivian Malone Jones. In 1965, she was the first African-American to graduate from The University of Alabama. She was given an honorary doctorate in humane letters from UA.

Who was the first woman to receive an MA from UA?

Lida McMahon, in 1902.

What UA alum went on to direct orchestras in places like the Coconut Grove and the Armando Club?

Buddy Clark, who was known at UA as Herbert Kreisberg, class of 1937.

What UA alum and physician was a pioneer in the use of X-rays?

Dr. Eugene Northington, whose work with the Roentgen ray helped aid the suffering of others, but in turn caused his demise. Northington General Hospital was named in his honor.

What two UA alums helped implement the Civil Rights Act of 1964 and the Voting Rights Act of 1965?

Founders of the Southern Poverty Law Center Morris Dees and Joseph J. Levin Jr.

What online open-source encyclopedia was invented by UA graduate Jimmy Wales?

Wikipedia.

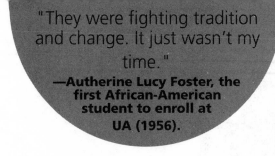

In 1987, what did UA graduate Morris Dees and his Southern Poverty Law Center accomplish for client Beulah Mae Donald?

They argued her case against the Klansmen who had lynched her son, Michael, in 1981, and when she won, the courts awarded her $7 million to be paid by The United Klans of America. Since the Klan had nowhere near that amount of money to turn over to Mrs. Donald, she ended up bankrupting the organization and possessing their Alabama headquarters building.

Tom Cherones, who received his MA in broadcast and flm communication at UA, directed over 80 episodes of which popular 1990s sitcom?

Seinfeld.

Leaders

Who was the first president of The University of Alabama? Where was he from?

Alva Woods (1831-1837) Vermont—though he was educated in Massachusetts, at Phillips Academy and at Harvard.

What UA president served as the chaplain at the inauguration of Jefferson Davis on February 18, 1861?

Basil Manly (1837-1855). Manly was an ardent secessionist.

Upon leaving his post after eighteen years of presidency, what other "Alabama" and "Southern" institutions did Manly help deveop?

The Southern Baptist Convention, the Alabama Historical Society, and the Alabama Insane Hospital (later known as Bryce Hospital).

What UA president is believed to have started UA's first musical group?

Landon Cabell Garland (1855-1865). Family tradition says that Garland organized a musical group soon after joining the faculty as a professor in 1847.

Name the UA president who was member of the University's inaugural class, attending UA from 1831 to 1834.

William Russell Smith (1870-1871).

Which former UA president was the father of the first Auburn football team captain?

Nathaniel Thomas Lupton (1871-1874).

"The University is the Capstone of higher education in Alabama."

—Dr. George Hutchinson Denny

What former UA president was known to have had three horses shot out from under him at Jonesboro during the Civil War? What prompted him to come to The University of Alabama?

Henry DeLamar Clayton (1886-1889). An unsuccessful bid for the governorship of Alabama. He came to UA to teach international law. He was conferred with an honorary degree of doctor of laws before taking his teaching post.

What UA president was the first University graduate to hold the office of president? What major accomplishments occurred during his presidency?

Burwell Boykin Lewis (1880-1885). He graduated from The University of Alabama in 1857. He was responsible for bringing in funds from the US Congress for war losses, and for rebuilding the campus both physically and psychologically following the Civil War.

In what area did Burwell Boykin Lewis teach?

Constitutional law.

What UA president served less than a year but was renowned as a naval officer and hydrographer, and inventor of the electric torpedo?

Mathew Fontaine Maury. He served only briefly as president in the latter half of 1871.

Which UA professor studied under a famed chemist whose name is immortalized in a piece of chemistry equipment used in every lab around the world?

Nathaniel Thomas Lupton (1871-1874)—he studied in Germany under Robert Wilhelm Bunsen, namesake of the "Bunsen burner."

What 19th-century UA president left the University to become president of the Normal College for Girls at Livingston (now the University of West Alabama)?

Carlos G. Smith (1874-1878). The Board of Trustees voted not to reappoint him in 1878 and brought about great public controversy.

What UA president served as acting president multiple times before finally accepting the post permanently?

William Stokes Wyman, in 1879-80, 1885-86 and in 1889-90. He accepted the appointment as UA president in 1901.

What screen legend was photographed with UA President Richard Clarke Foster on the 1938 Rose Bowl trip?

Humphrey Bogart.

What former UA president served as supervisor of campus construction before becoming president and saw a major building program that continued throughout his tenure as president?

John Morin Gallalee (1948-1953)—nine dormitories, two classroom buildings and a stadium expansion occurred during his tenure.

What two former UA presidents also served as chancellors of Vanderbilt University?

Landon Cabell Garland and Oliver Cromwell Carmichael. Garland is buried on the Vanderbilt campus.

Which president saw the admission of women to The University of Alabama?

Richard Channing Jones (1890-1897).

During the creation of an 1852 map of the UA campus, who served as "chain bearer"?

Then-President Basil Manly. He was directly involved in the measuring of campus to ensure the accuracy of the map.

What UA administrator served as the Dean of Men during the integration of The University of Alabama in 1963?

John L. Blackburn. A UA institute is named in his honor.

What former UA president launched the "Greater University Building Program," which resulted in the first construction on campus in nearly two decades? What other major endeavor occurred during his tenure?

John William Abercrombie (1902-1911). This plan was launched in 1906. He instituted summer school for teachers at UA, which began in 1904.

Where were the first summer school courses taught?

Outside, under canopies. Enrollment was so great during the second session that many of the male students lived in university-provided tents on campus.

What was the name of Dr. Denny's beloved dog?

Bonnie.

What wife of a former UA president penned a book on the President's Mansion, written from the point of view of the mansion?

Mary Mathews, wife of Dr. David Mathews.

> "Keep your head up; act like a champion."
> **—Bear Bryant**

What interesting rule was stated in the UA Board of Trustees Oath of Office, written in 1848?

It states that the Trustees were forbidden to take up arms against each other, or against State Officials.

Which UA president came to Alabama after a brilliant thirty-five year career with the University of Texas system?

President Robert E. Witt. His tenure in Texas included ten years as dean of the business school at the University of Texas at Austin, and eight years as president of the University of Texas at Arlington.

What rank did UA President Josiah Gorgas hold in the CSA? When Gorgas resigned as seventh president of The University of Alabama in 1879, what University post was awarded to him?

Brigadier-General. University librarian.

Who was the youngest president of The University of Alabama? What prestigious position did he accept in 1975 which required him to leave Tuscaloosa for three years?

> "Bryant was a man who embodied our national character. I was a great fan of his. "
> **—Ronald Reagan**

Dr. David Mathews, who served from 1969 to 1980, and was just thirty-four when he became president. He was named the US Secretary of Health, Education and Welfare under President Ford's administration.

What UA president had been the youngest university president in American history?

Dr. Frank Rose (1958-1969), who was president of Transylvania University in Kentucky at age 30.

What other UA president also served as president of Transylvania University?

UA's first president—Alva Woods (1831-1837).

What current UA assistant vice president is an internationally recognized poet?

Dr. Hank Lazer. His works have been published in leading magazines and journals.

What UA dean wrote the definitive work on the integration of The University of Alabama?

Dean E. Culpepper Clark, author of *Schoolhouse Door: Segregation's Last Stand at The University of Alabama* (Oxford University Press, 1993).

Why segregation's "last stand"?

Alabama was the fiftieth state in the union to integrate its public school system.

Under what president were doctoral degrees first offered at UA?

President John M. Gallalee.

What programs offered the first PhD degrees?

Commerce and business administration, chemistry, education, English, biology, history, physics, political science, anatomy, biochemistry, pharmacology, and physiology.

What University of Alabama president served at two separate times and later became chancellor?

Dr. Denny. He first served The University of Alabama from 1912 to 1937, and then returned upon the death of President Foster in 1941.

The Hoole Library is named for whom?

William Stanley Hoole. Besides directing the University libraries for many years, he authored several books and articles in a myriad of areas, with a special interest in Southern history.

Which university president was responsible for turning The University of Alabama into a military school? In what year? What were his motivations?

President Landon Cabell Garland. 1860, though Garland had begun to make plans for the conversion in 1854. An attempt to control student behavior.

Who was sometimes called the "Angel of the Campus Cadets"? What distinction did she receive in Washington as a young woman?

Amelia Gayle Gorgas. She was one of two women on the platform during the ceremony when the cornerstone of the Washington Monument was laid.

What former UA administrative leader single-handedly acquired Moundville to be part of The University of Alabama?

Dr. Walter B. Jones, who at the time was Alabama's state geologist, purchased the land with his own money to assure that it would be saved and studied.

What UA administrative leader received two major honors relating to Alabama in 2003?

> Dr. Malcolm Portera, chancellor of The University of Alabama system. In 2003, he was inducted into the Alabama Academy of Honor, and also the Governor's Award for Distinguished Service to Alabama by Governor Bob Riley.

From what institution did Dr. Denny come to The University of Alabama?

> He came from Washington and Lee College in 1912, where he had served as president.

Who was The University of Alabama's first Rhodes Scholar? What major milestone occurred during his presidency?

> Oliver Cromwell Carmichael, who went on to graduate from UA in 1911 and return in 1953 as president of the University until 1957. He was president when Autherine Lucy, the first African-American student to be admitted to UA, came to campus in 1956.

What former UA president was a captain in the Creek War and served in the Congress of the Confederacy as well as the U.S. Congress?

William Russell Smith, who served as UA president briefly in 1870-71.

What year did Lee Bidgood, namesake of Bidgood Hall, begin his role as director of the School of Commerce and Business Administration? What other administrative role did he take on in 1953?

1919. He served as interim president upon the retirement of President Gallalee.

In what language were the earliest university diplomas written, including the names of the students and faculty?

Latin.

"We, as teachers, coaches, administrators, and students must understand that success will be determined largely by the hard work, communication and sacrifice for each other. We are accountable to each other in the classroom, on the playing field, and in the community."

—UA head football coach Mike Shula

When was the graduate school first established?

It was established in 1922 and instituted in 1924.

Who was the first dean of the Graduate School?

Dr. A.B. Moore.

Who was the first dean of the law school?

Dean Albert J. Farrah. Farrah Hall, the former Law School building, bears his name.

What two former UA presidents were honored as one of the "Ten Outstanding Young Men in America"?

Dr. Rose, in 1954, and Dr. Mathews, in 1969.

What did students raise money for after the death of president Foster in 1941?

An iron lung—students raised more than $1,200 for an iron lung to be donated to Druid City Hospital in Dr. Foster's name.

What UA president was elected as the president of the State University Association?

President Paty (1942-1947) was elected to that post in 1943.

During President Paty's early years as president, why was the campus so crowded? Why did he leave UA?

Despite low enrollment during wartime, throughout 1943 and 1944, UA housed, fed and trained—both academically and physically—almost 13,000 men in US army and navy programs. To accept the chancellorship at the University of Georgia system.

How many female students were there when Dr. Denny became president in 1912?

Fifty-five.

Thirty-three years later, how many women were on campus?

Enrollment for the 1944-45 academic years shows 1,508 female students.

What former dean of women and dean of the College of Home economics was conferred with a LLD degree by the University in 1941 in recognition for her more than three decades of service to UA?

Dean Agnes Ellen Harris.

When was The University of Alabama system created?

In 1975.

When was the Honors College first established at UA? Who was named its first dean?

In September 2003. Dr. Robert Halli, who oversees its three divisions: University Honors, Computer-based Honors, and International Honors.

What administrative body oversaw the creation of the System?

The University of Alabama's Board of Trustees.

"They all came to Alabama because they wanted a great education, they wanted to be part of a family environment and they all wanted to win a national championship."

—UA women's gymnastics head coach Sarah Patterson, on her 2002 national championship team

Who was the first woman to serve on UA's Board of Trustees?

Martha Simms—she was confirmed as a trustee by the Alabama state legislature in 1981.

What current UA administrator penned a poignant poem to mark the fortieth anniversary of the integration of The University of Alabama? What did he do to the benefit of the UA community and to Tuscaloosa and Northport?

Dr. Charles Ray Nash, vice chancellor for academic affairs for The University of Alabama system. His poem is entitled "Our Future." Dr. Nash initiated the application for Tuscaloosa-Northport to be designated an All-America City, which it received in 2002.

Before being named provost in 2003, what UA college did Provost Judy Bonner serve as dean for fourteen years?

> Dean of the College of Human Environmental Sciences.

What former UA president was instrumental in the establishment of Alabama Institute for Manufacturing Excellence (AIME).

> Dr. Roger Sayers (1988-1996).

What former UA president was the uncle of a legend in UA sports broadcasting?

> President Richard Clarke Foster—his nephew John Forney was known to many as the "Voice of the Crimson Tide."

Who was the first chancellor of The University of Alabama system? What other administrative first did he achieve?

> Joseph F. Volker, who became chancellor in 1976. He was the UA's first dean of the School of Dentistry.

When was the Department of Fine Arts officially formed? Who was the first director of the then-newly formed Department of Fine Arts?

In 1943. Dr. Alton O'Steen. The new department combined art, music and related fields.

What UA alum and administrator was inducted into the prestigious Alabama Academy of Honor in 2004? What other honor do they both share?

Dr. Cathy Johnson Randall. Dr. Randall was nominated for the honor by Harper Lee, fellow UA alum and honoree. The Academy is limited to 100 living Alabamians plus living governors, and vacancies occur only at the death of a member. Both Randall and Lee have been named among the University's "XXXI Most Outstanding Women Graduates of the Century."

"During my initial visit to UA it became clear that here was the combination I had been hoping to find -- outstanding librarians, dedicated staff, and administrators who acknowledge that libraries are central to providing quality higher education."

—Dr. Louis A. Pitschmann, UA's Dean of Libraries

Which of UA's presidents was also a biology professor and co-author of naturalism books including *Wildflowers of Alabama and Adjoining States*?

Dr. Joab Thomas (1981-1988).

Which wife of a former UA president has an endowed fund named in her honor, created to strengthen the University libraries' collections on women?

Donna Sorensen Endowed Libraries Collection, named for the wife of former UA president Dr. Andrew Sorensen.

Town and Gown

What Tuscaloosa native won a Grammy award in 1959?

Dinah Washington—the song was "What a Diff'rence a Day Makes!" Washington was born in Tuscaloosa in 1924, but left at age four and moved to Chicago with her family.

What former UA student became the youngest city councilperson in Tuscaloosa history?

Lee Garrison—he was elected in August 1997 while still an undergraduate at UA for City Council, District 4.

"He never knew pain who never felt the pangs of love."
-Samuel P. Thomas, Class of 1906

What was located on McFarland Boulevard between Hargrove Road and Veteran's Memorial Parkway before University Mall was built?

Military barracks and Northington General Hospital—one of the premier hospitals in the country for treating burn victims, at one time.

What was unique about Northington Hospital when it opened in 1944?

It was the second-largest hospital in the United States.

What was Northington Hospital's fate?

It was blown up on film.

What film was this explosion used for? What world's record was broken during the filming of that movie?

Hooper (1978), starring Burt Reynolds and Sally Field. The last few minutes were filmed at Northington. A.J. Bakunas, stunt man for Burt Reynolds (who ironically was playing a stunt man in the film), dropped 232 feet, setting a record for the highest jump without a parachute.

What other film that captures fictional life in Tuscaloosa starred Sally Field?

Forrest Gump (1994).

What Tuscaloosa establishment's nickname is a reflection of the travel time it takes to get there?

Nick's—known affectionately as "Nick's in the Sticks."

What is the specialty drink of the house at Nick's?

A Nicodemus—bright red and very strong!

What distinction did Tuscaloosa receive in 2002? In what company was Tuscaloosa for this award?

It was named an "All-America City." Anchorage, Alaska; Fountain, Colorado; Elgin, Illinois; Roswell, New Mexico; Buffalo-Niagara, New York; Huntington, New York; Weslaco, Texas; Hampton, Virginia; and Everett, Washington were also chosen.

What popular Tuscaloosa restaurant, now situated on McFarland Boulevard across from Snow Hinton Park, was first located on The Strip when it opened in 1980?

Manna Grocery and Deli.

What presently unused structure in Tuscaloosa was designed by a student of famed architect Frank Lloyd Wright?

Queen City Pool, located on Jack Warner Parkway (formerly River Road). Its unique round design is unmistakably influenced by the Wright's Prairie Style architecture.

What Tuscaloosa native became Alabama's first and only female governor?

Lurleen B. Wallace. She was also the first and only spouse of a former Alabama governor to become governor of Alabama.

Whose motto is "Ain't Nothin' Like 'em Nowhere"?

Dreamland Barbeque.

What is the oldest church in Tuscaloosa County? What significance does this church hold to The University of Alabama?

First Baptist Church in Tuscaloosa. It was first organized in 1818, and the first buildings were constructed of logs. The church was influenced by the leadership of the first two UA presidents, Alva Woods and Basil Manly, who both often filled the pulpit.

What world-class art collection is on display in Tuscaloosa?

The Westervelt-Warner Museum of American Art, a collection of more than 400 works by such artists as Whistler, Homer, Cassatt and many others. The museum was built in 2003 to showcase the impressive collection of paintings, sculpture, artifacts and antiques collected by Tuscaloosa native and Gulf States Paper Co. CEO Jack Warner.

Why is Tuscaloosa known as "The Druid City"?

The name is derived from the presence of many large oak trees in the city. In ancient times the Druids held the oak tree in great reverence and conducted their rituals in oak forests.

Where did Tuscaloosa get its name?

The modern city name, "Tuscaloosa," was derived from the old name, "Tuskaloosa." In the languages of the Creek and Choctaw Indians, "tushka" means warrior and "lusa" means black.

What is the name of the river that runs through the city?

The Black Warrior River!

What downtown Tuscaloosa church was built in 1829, making it the second oldest of its denomination in the state of Alabama? What is its significance to The University of Alabama?

Christ Episcopal Church, organized January 7, 1828. Charter ceremonies for UA were held in this church and Reverend Alva Woods was installed as first president of the University on April 12, 1831.

Name the bookstore once located on the Strip that was named for a Tom Robbins novel.

Another Roadside Attraction—it closed in the 1980s.

What Tuscaloosa community leader was the first African-American elected to the Tuscaloosa County Commission?

Joseph W. Mallisham.

What once stood on the site of Snow Hinton Park? Who is the park named for?

Northington General Hospital. Former Tuscaloosa mayor Snow Hinton.

Name the man who won a Pulitzer Prize for speaking out against segregation in Tuscaloosa in 1956.

Buford Boone, editor and publisher of the *Tuscaloosa News*. His editorial "What a Price for Peace" was published on February 7, 1956.

"If I should go to sleep for 61 years and wake up in the middle of the Sahara dessert I would feel no more lost than I do now, coming back to UA after 61 years absence."

—Joseph U. Gillespie, class of 1873 remarking on the changes to the UA

What Tuscaloosa church is the oldest Black Presbyterian church in Alabama?

The Brown Memorial Presbyterian Church. It was organized by Dr. Charles A. Stillman as Salem Church in December 1880.

What Tuscaloosa facility was designed using what is called moral architecture? When was it established? What internationally known humanitarian aided in its establishment?

Bryce Hospital, originally called the Alabama Insane Hospital. Alabama was the first state to appropriate sufficient funds for such a facility. In 1852, and it opened in 1861. The linear architecture of the main building of what was to become known as Bryce Hospital served as a model for dozens of mental institutions across the United States. Dorothea Dix.

What is the oldest scientific agency in the state of Alabama?

The Geological Survey of Alabama, which was established by legislative mandate in 1848. Its offices are on the UA campus.

Who built the first bridge spanning the Black Warrior River between Tuscaloosa and Northport?

The first was built in 1834 by Horace King, who at that time, was enslaved. King engineered the third bridge in 1872. He had been freed in 1846 and had become a well-known bridge builder in Alabama and Georgia.

What happened to the first bridge? What was the fate of the second bridge?

It was destroyed by a tornado in 1842. Built in 1852, it was defended by Tuscaloosa Home Guard before its destruction by Federal troops in April 1865.

What innovation in 1943 made travel to the capital much easier?

The opening of the "University Highway"—now US 82—a route that connected Montgomery to Tuscaloosa and took approximately fifty miles off of the trip between the two cities.

What manufacturing facility in Tuscaloosa is the largest of its kind outside of its native country?

> The Mercedes-Benz plant, which was established in Tuscaloosa in 1994 and underwent a $600 million expansion in 2000. It is one of the largest employers in Alabama.

What's the Crazy Bucket?

> A signature drink at famed Tuscaloosa watering hole Harry's Bar.

What former U.S. congressman and U.S. ambassador to New Zealand, Fiji, Tonga and Western Samoa once practiced law in Tuscaloosa?

> Armistead Selden Jr.

What corporation headquartered in Tuscaloosa was founded in 1884?

> Gulf States Paper Corporation. It is one of the nation's largest privately held forest products companies.

Who started his first newspaper, *The Alabama Citizen*, in Tuscaloosa in 1943 and soon became one of Alabama's preeminent newspaper publishers?

Frank Thomas. In 1972, Thomas was the first African-American inducted into the Alabama Newspaper Hall of Honor in recognition of his efforts to promote the advancement of civil rights, understanding and racial harmony in Alabama.

What Tuscaloosa institution opened in 1956 and closed its doors for the last time on Halloween of 2003? What words were painted outside iy for many years?

The Chukker. "Liberté, Egalité, Fraternité! Vive le Chukker—1956."

"My feelings have changed through the years, as I have watched UA push forward in the enrollment and graduation of African-American students, to the point that today it is a national leader among doctoral degree granting institutions. I have admired even more UA's awareness that it is not where it needs and wants to be on the issues that vitally affect the people of this state, especially its African-American population. But I have confidence today, that I would not have had years ago, that it will succeed."

—**Vivian Malone Jones, first African-American graduate of UA, 2000 UA Commencement address.**

Name the Tuscaloosa city councilperson who hosts a daily television program. What annual fundraiser takes place where his show is taped, and also appears on local TV?

Kip Tyner—his show is *Great Day Tuscaloosa!* The Mall Ball, an Easter Seals fundraiser, takes place annually in McFarland Mall.

What other major fundraiser takes place in Tuscaloosa annually, raising thousands for WAAO, (West Alabama Aids Outreach)? When does it take place?

The annual Bal Masque. During Mardi Gras season, just before Fat Tuesday.

What "local meat and three" has fried green tomatoes only on Tuesdays and Thursdays?

City Café—A downtown Northport staple that has been feeding hungry UA students and the Tuscaloosa community for over thirty years.

What Tuscaloosa restaurant chain celebrated its thirtieth anniversary in 2004?

Taco Casa—known not only for its great food, but also for its great ice.

What annual event unites the University community and the Tuscaloosa community to celebrate spring?

The annual Sakura Festival—Sakura is a Japapnese festival of cherry blossoms, and has been celebrated in Tusacloosa since 1986. It is organized by the Japan Program, part of UA's Capstone International Programs.

What Japanese manufacturing corporation has a plant in Tusacloosa?

JVC. The people at JVC were instrumental in establishing the Sakura Festival.

What self-proclaimed UA football "head" cheerleader ran for public office thirteen times, including several bids for governor, and lost them all? What was the name of his book, published in 1980?

Short Price. *Shorty: I Ain't Nothing but a Loser.*

What major newspaper company now owns the Tuscaloosa News?

The New York Times.

Campus

What was the first permanent structure on The University of Alabama campus? In what year was it built?

The Gorgas House. 1828, as part of the original master plan for The University of Alabama.

Who designed the original architectural plan for the campus of The University of Alabama?

William Nichols.

From what two campuses did Nichols gain inspiration?

> From Thomas Jefferson's design for the University of Virginia, as well as his own work on the campus for the University of North Carolina-Chapel Hill.

What is the only structure on campus that survives from the 1828 master plan of architect William Nichols?

> The Gorgas House.

What was the first function of what is now known as the Gorgas House? What was the Gorgas House built with?

> It was originally called "the hotel" and was a dining hall for students. Bricks. These bricks had been used as ballast for English ships that sailed to America and then returned home with Alabama cotton.

When did the Gorgas House first become associated with the Gorgas family? For how many years did a member of the Gorgas family live in this building?

In 1879, when Josiah Gorgas resigned as seventh University of Alabama president due to poor health, he and his family moved into what was then called the "Pratt House" rent-free. Sixty-five years. The last surviving child of the Gorgases, Maria Gorgas, lived in the house until 1954.

What was the first campus building to be completed after the Civil War?

"The Barracks"—now known as Woods Hall, named for first UA President Alva Woods. It uses many bricks salvaged from the original campus buildings.

In what year was Morgan Hall built?

1911.

"He set a standard of excellence here in that some say is too high but in my opinion that's not necessarily a bad thing. If you don't play football or any other sport to win, you're not much of a competitor. Yet, team spirit and character are extremely important in athletics but in the end cut through all the clichés and we all play the game to win."

—**Bryant Museum director Ken Gaddy on Bear Bryant**

In what year did The University of Alabama first begin offering summer school?

1904.

How does The University of Alabama compare in terms of enrollment with other campuses across the state of Alabama? What percentage of that number were Alabama natives?

It is by far the largest, with more than 20,000 students enrolled in fall 2004. 75 percent.

How many foreign countries are represented in The University of Alabama's student enrollment?

Seventy-nine countries other than the United States.

How many Rhodes Scholars have come from The University of Alabama.

Fifteen.

What Alabama Museum of Natural History produced program was nominated for an Emmy award in 2005?

Discovering Alabama. Dr. Doug Phillips, originator, producer and host of the series, and Roger Reid, production coordinator, are nominated for their efforts in developing the episode entitled "Black Belt, Part I."

In what year did The University of Alabama open?

1831.

In what year was Denny Chimes built and dedicated?

1929.

What is special about the trees that line University Boulevard along the side of the Quad?

These trees were planted as a memorial in 1921 by the Tuscaloosa post of the American Legion for those from Tuscaloosa who died in World War I. The plaques are gone, but the trees are registered with the National Forestry Service in Washington DC.

What was the "Union Building"?

Now known as Reese-Phifer Hall, and used by the College of Communication and Information Sciences, the Union Building was built and dedicated in 1930 as "a memorial to all former University of Alabama students who have borne arms in defense of their country."

On what other facility was the original Denny Stadium modeled?

The Yale Bowl.

How many seats did the original stadium hold?

12,072.

What did students do when they saw the elderly Gorgas sisters?

Men would bow and women would curtsey.

What two women were credited with rescuing campus buildings from the fires set by Federal troops in 1865?

Mrs. Landon Garland, who saved the President's Mansion (which was her family's home), and Mrs. Reuben Chapman, who pleaded for the Observatory to be spared.

Name the four buildings that survived the burning by Union troops.

The Gorgas House, the Observatory, the President's Mansion and the Little Round House.

What distinction did the Observatory have?

It was the largest observatory east of the Mississippi.

Who were "Miss Julia's Girls"?

Members of the first class of resident women.

When was the first residence hall for women opened?

In 1899—called the Julia Tutwiler Annex, it housed just ten female students.

Who was the guest performer at the first Rev. Dr. Martin Luther King Jr. Memorial "Realizing the Dream" Concert in 1989?

The actor James Earl Jones.

Who is buried in the University's cemetery?

At least two enslaved individuals, named Jack and Boysey, both listed as belonging to then-President Basil Manly; a student, William J. Crawford, who died of typhus fever in 1844; and family of former UA professor Horace S. Pratt. Another student, Samuel James, was buried there in 1839, but his body was later disinterred.

Which glam rocker, one of the first openly homosexual rock stars, performed his last concert (to four encores) in 1974 in Morgan Auditorium?

Jobriath (born Bruce Wayne Campbell), a primary influence on the glam rock characters depicted in the 1998 movie *The Velvet Goldmine*.

Which 1995 movie with a title referencing The University of Alabama starred Denzel Washington, Gene Hackman and a submarine?

Crimson Tide.

Why did the movie have that name?

Because the submarine it depicts is the USS *Alabama*. The captain of the submarine also has a dog named Bear, after you-know-who.

What 2002 film featured a character whose pet was named for Coach Bryant? What other celebrity animal named "Bear" was named after Coach Bryant?

Sweet Home Alabama. That "Bear" was the chimp in the 1970s hit TV show *B.J. and the Bear*—it was revealed on an episode that B.J. named his pal in honor of the legendary UA football coach Bear Bryant.

"My feelings have changed through the years, as I have watched UA push forward in the enrollment and graduation of African-American students, to the point that today it is a national leader among doctoral degree granting institutions. I have admired even more UA's awareness that it is not where it needs and wants to be on the issues that vitally affect the people of this state, especially its African-American population. But I have confidence today, that I would not have had years ago, that it will succeed."

—Vivian Malone Jones, first African-American graduate of UA, 2000 UA Commencement address.

According to Alabama folklorist Kathryn Tucker Windham, whose ghost haunts Smith Hall, which houses the Alabama Museum of Natural History?

The founder of the museum and namesake of the building, geologist Eugene Allen Smith (1841-1927), is said to visit from time to time.

When was the military structure of the University abolished?

March 3, 1903. This was initiated by a rebellion that took place in December of 1900 where most of the students enrolled at UA demanded the removal of the military structure.

How many telephones were there on campus in 1955?

321.

When was the President's Mansion erected? How much did it cost to build?

1841. $18,000.

When were women first enrolled at UA? What was their status that first year?

The fall of 1893. They were considered "special students" rather than regular students.

Who were the first two female students?

Miss Anna Byrne Adams and Miss Bessie Parker, both from Tuscaloosa.

By 1900, how many female students were enrolled at UA?

Twenty-eight.

Who was the leading crusader to make The University of Alabama co-educational? Who was her father?

Julia S. Tutwiler. Henry Tutwiler, one of the first professors hired for the opening of The University of Alabama.

What did Professor Tutwiler teach?

Ancient languages.

"These students will remain on campus. They will register today. They will go to school tomorrow."

—Deputy Attorney General Nicholas Katzenbach, in reference to Vivian Malone and James Hood, to George Wallace at Foster Auditorium, 1963

When did men and women first live together in the same dorm complex on campus?

In the fall of 1970—Mary Burke Hall East was converted to a men's dorm, and Mary Burke West remained a women's dorm.

When The University of Alabama was founded in 1831, what was the population of what was then known as Tuskaloosa?

1,068 people inhabited the area, which was accessible only by roads and by water. There was no railroad at the time.

How many locations were considered for The University of Alabama?

Twelve originally, and five in the final ballot (Tuscaloosa, Montevallo, Lagrange, Athens, Belfont). Tuscaloosa received 47 out of 81 votes from the state legislature.

What was the name of the chosen site?

The chosen site for The University of Alabama campus was known as Marr's Spring, located on what was known in the 1820s as Huntsville Road.

Who was Marr's Spring named for?

A major, or Judge Marr, who occupied and farmed the land that was to become the campus. He lived in a house where Gorgas House now stands. Marr's Spring still exists on campus behind the Ferguson Center and near ten Hoor Hall.

Where were the materials acquired for the first UA campus buildings?

Sandstone was quarried locally, some bricks were made on site and the lumber was milled from UA's own timber tract.

What is the claim to fame of the Hodges Meteorite, on display at UA's Alabama Museum of Natural History?

It is the only meteorite known to have struck a human being (Ann Elizabeth Hodges of Sylacauga, Alabama). She sustained a large bruise on her hip, but no permanent physical damage.

Which legendary rock star started his 1990
UA homecoming concert in Coleman
Coliseum by announcing that since he was
in Alabama, he should sing some Hank
Williams?

Bob Dylan.

Which Hank Williams song did he
perform?

"Hey Good Lookin'."

How often do Denny Chimes sound? What tune do
the chimes play? How many steps are there in Denny
Chimes? How many flights of stairs?

Every fifteen minutes. "Westminster Peal," the same as
Big Ben in London. Ninety-two. Thirteen.

When was air conditioning first installed on campus?
What building had the first air conditioning?

August 1953. Gorgas Library.

"I must down to the seas again, for the call of the running tide is a wild call and a clear call that must not be denied."

—John Masefield (1878-1967), from "Sea Fever"

What was the original appropriation of funds for the first University of Alabama Library?

$6,000 in 1830. It was the largest library in the South prior to the Civil War.

Name the first student officially enrolled in The University of Alabama.

Silas L. Gunn.

How many students were enrolled when UA first opened?

Fifty-two.

How many professors were on hand to teach them?

Four.

When was the ceremony held to open The University of Alabama? Where was it held?

April 12, 1831. Christ Episcopal Church in downtown Tuscaloosa.

How did the ceremony culminate?

Alabama Governor Samuel B. Moore spoke and then delivered the keys to The University of Alabama to Alva Woods, UA's first president.

Where was The University of Alabama School of Medicine originally located?

Mobile.

What degree program at UA, which started in 1985, is the only one of its kind in the world?

The MFA in the book arts program. This program, which teaches printing, publishing, bookbinding, papermaking and the history of the book, is internationally known and respected.

What seated US president visited the UA campus as part of an election campaign? Where did he eat lunch after his speech?

Ronald Reagan—who visited on October 15, 1984 as part of his re-election campaign tour. He spoke to 9,000 people on the UA campus. McDonalds in Northport. He had a Big Mac, large fries and an iced tea.

What myth is represented on the 18th-century wallpaper at the University Club?

Cupid and Psyche.

When did UA first offer "distance education"?

In 1919, with the founding of the Extension Division.

"UA is proud of its alumni. Day by day, all over this nation and on the battlefronts of the world, the sons and daughters of the University are adding greatly to its glory through distinguished careers of social usefulness."

—Raymond R. Paty, UA president, 1943

What UA campus building was designated a National Historic Landmark in 2005? What two major campus activities took place there for decades?

Foster Auditorium, the site of George Wallace's "Stand" and the place where Vivian Malone and James Hood registered for classes in June 1963, finally integrating The University of Alabama. Registration and graduation—the first and last campus career milestones.

What other activities took place in Foster?

It was designed as a multipurpose facility, and it has been just that—concerts, dances, sporting events and lectures have all taken place there over the years.

When was Foster Auditorium constructed?

1939.

What do Gorgas Library and Foster Auditorium have in common? How was this accomplished?

They are both WPA buildings—constructed as part of President Roosevelt's New Deal. Very few campus buildings were built as WPA projects. Dr. Denny, along with Dr. Foster and the future US senator from Florida and UA alum visited Roosevelt in the White house, and explained that UA needed a library because the old one was "burned by the Yankees." UA eventually got the funding.

How was this story disseminated?

By President Roosevelt himself, who regaled America with the tale during one of his famous fireside chats.

What was Emphasis? What was the Emphasis controversy of 1970?

A student-organized speaker series that ran successfully in the late 1960s and early 1970s. Speakers included Robert F. Kennedy, William Kuntzler, Dick Gregory and Madalyn Murray O'Hair. Controversial speakers were banned from campus—Abbie Hoffman, of the infamous Chicago Seven, was banned from speaking alongside George Wallace. A court battle ensued.

What was "Experimental College"?

A student-run college at UA that offered free courses, including classes in soccer, folk, rock, blues, euthanasia and much more. Nearly 1,000 students took these classes.

What was "Little Bo"?

The snack bar on the ground floor of Woods Hall.

What was the first Greek letter fraternity to establish a chapter at UA? Where were the first members initiated?

Delta Kappa Epsilon, in 1847. They were initiated at the old Indian Queen Hotel by Charles Foote of DKE's Phi chapter at Yale College.

What is the nickname for the DKE house?

Built in 1916, it is known as "The Mansion on the Hill."

What was the first Greek letter sorority to establish a UA chapter? What other firsts does this sorority hold?

Kappa Delta, in 1904. The Zeta chapter of Kappa Delta is the first sorority to have a chapter in the state of Alabama. It is now the oldest continuous KD Chapter in the United States.

What is missing from the current Julia Tutwiler Hall?

The thirteenth floor.

What is the name of the campus center at The University of Alabama? Who is the building named for? What was he best known for on campus?

The Ferguson Center. Hill Ferguson, who received degrees from UA in 1896 and 1897. Besides playing football as a student and working as the business manager for the *Corolla*, he spent a record forty years as a member of The University of Alabama's Board of Trustees, retiring from the board in 1959.

When was the Ferguson Center completed?

1973.

What campus dormitory was destroyed by fire in January 1935? Who was the building named for?

Gorgas Hall. General William Crawford Gorgas, the son of Amelia and Josiah Gorgas.

What is General William Crawford Gorgas best known for? Besides saving countless lives, what monumental engineering achievement was completed due to Gorgas's medical work?

As a medical doctor and surgeon general for the U.S. army, he was largely responsible for the eradication of yellow fever, an overwhelming killer in the 19th century. The completion of the Panama Canal.

When did UA's College of Commerce and Business Administration begin?

In January 1920. Within one year, 167 students were enrolled in business courses at UA.

What fraternity, now the largest social fraternity in North America, was founded on The University of Alabama campus in 1956? What is the fraternity's nickname?

Sigma Alpha Epsilon. "Mother Mu".

What is the "Order of the Coif"?

A prestigious national academic honor society for legal education. UA's was established in 1970.

What groundbreaking UA college was founded that same year?

New College—under then-President David Mathews.

What is New College?

Begun as an experiment, it is an innovative and successful interdisciplinary college for motivated and intelligent students at UA, which allows them to develop their own major and take control over their course work and educational path.

"My football training under Wade, plus my experience since boyhood in the hunting and outdoor life of Alabama are undoubtedly responsible for the fact I am alive today."

—Hugh Barr Miller, class of 1932, on his miraculous rescue after the sinking of the destroyer The Strong in 1943

Name the prestigious "writers series" held at UA. What was the quad sometimes used for during the years 1893-1914?

The Bankhead Writers Series, endowed by the Bankhead Foundation. It was the site of Alabama football games before the University Field was established.

In what year was the first section of Denny Stadium completed?

1929. It opened on September 28 of that year.

What was the seating capacity when it opened?

12,000 people.

In what year was the stadium renamed Bryant-Denny?

Coach Bryant's name was added in 1975.

As of fall 2004, what was the seating capacity in Bryant-Denny Stadium? How many seat were added in 2005?

83,818 seats—more than enough to provide a seat for every man, woman and child in the city limits (79,294, according to a 2003 US census estimate)! 10,000 more seats, bringing its capacity to well over 90,000!

What building on campus was evacuated to house the National Defense League?

Woods Hall. It was converted after Dunkirk, in 1941.

What was cut by 30 percent on campus in 1941?

Power—as a war effort to conserve energy, power was cut off on campus from 7:30 p.m. until 4:30 a.m. each day.

What was "Mad Wednesday"? What stunning outcome of "Mad Wednesday" marked a first on campus?

May 13, 1970, was a day of conflict on campus between pro- and anti-administration students. Final exams were made optional.

In what year were the Department of Radio and the Department of Journalism combined?

They were combined in 1973 to form what was then called the School of Communication, now known as the College of Communication and Information Sciences.

What was Dressler Hall? What was its fate?

An intramural sports building on campus. It burned to the ground during student demonstrations.

What other program, the only one of its kind in the state of Alabama, began in 1970?

The graduate program in Library and Information Studies—undergraduate work was already a long tradition in librarianship, but UA's master's program started in 1970.

What was the theme for the 125th Anniversary of The University of Alabama, held during the 1956-57 academic year?

Teaching, Research and Service.

When did UA become a military school? Which president devised this system for UA? What were his motivations for the change?

In 1860. President L.C. Garland. Garland had begun making plans and researching the military school system in 1854. To control unruly student behavior.

What was originally housed in the Rotunda? What was its fate? When was the Rotunda site discovered?

An auditorium on the first floor, and the campus library on the second floor. It was burned to the ground by Union troops in April 1865. In 1894, when workers were laying underground cable. The footprint of the building was just a few inches below ground level.

"When I arrived here, years of preparation had gone into making it happen. I had been active in my own community's efforts to end segregation. ... I then studied for two years at Alabama A&M, before answering the call that would lead me to the schoolhouse door at this University, where, two years later, I would become its first African-American graduate. Thirty-five years ago, by attending UA, I had the privilege of representing all those who fought for simple justice."

—Vivian Malone Jones, the first African-American graduate of UA

When did the burning of the UA campus take place?

On April 4, 1865—only five days before Lee's surrender at Appomattox.

What dubious distinction does The University of Alabama have that no other state university can claim?

It was the only one in the country to have been nearly destroyed by enemy action during wartime.

The charred remains of what three books were found in an excavation of the UA campus?

Shakespeare's *Much Ado About Nothing*, *Plane Geometry*, and *Geography of Africa*. The books were found where Madison Hall once stood.

What book was purported to have been rescued from the fire in the Rotunda when the campus was burned by federal troops in 1865? Was this really the only book that survived the fire? Who was the librarian at the time?

> An 1853 edition of the Koran. In 2005, the book was loaned to the Smithsonian for an exhibition. More than 1,200 library books survived from different parts of campus. Andre DeLoffre, who remained at his post through the invasion.

What was the Rotunda modeled after? On what classical building are both of these rotundas designed?

> William Nichols modeled it loosely after Thomas Jefferson's rotunda at the University of Virginia. They are based on the Roman Pantheon, which was constructed in AD 118-25.

Where is the only known photograph of the Rotunda and the antebellum campus housed? When was that photograph taken?

> In the W.S. Hoole Special Collections Library on the UA campus. It is believed to have been taken in 1859 and shows the Rotunda and two dormitories, along with a great deal of trees.

Where were classes first taught at UA?

The building called the Lyceum—the principal classroom building.

What were the names of the first dormitories?

Washington and Jefferson halls.

What exotic import landed on campus during WWII? Why were they in Tuscaloosa? What did many of them take home with them?

A detachment of more than 100 French cadets. To learn how to fly—they were selected from the French North African Army. Wives—by some accounts, more than eighty Alabama women married French cadets.

When did the Hillel Foundation establish its headquarters on the UA campus? Who was the first director of Hillel at UA?

In 1934. Rabbi Samuel Cook.

"It was a pleasure to pay on such a fine team as Alabama's."

—Bing Crosby, on losing several bets when his Stanford team lost to Alabama in the 1935 Rose Bowl

Name the UA handyman and janitor who worked with students for three decades, helping with their chemistry work, and on his own, experimented with developing fibers using local plants?

Sam S. May, known to students as "Dr. Sam," he worked at UA from 1911 until his death in 1941.

What program at UA was one of the first five of its kind in the United States?

Engineering. It began offering classes in 1837, just six years after the university opened its doors.

Name five novels that have depicted The University of Alabama.

Eating the Cheshire Cat by Helen Ellis; *Stars Fell on Alabama* by Carl Carmer; *Wonderdog* by Inman Majors; *Tuscaloosa* by W. Glasgow Phillips; and *Forrest Gump* by Winston Groom.

"I'm at a stage in my career [where] I'm not looking for a stepping stone to my next job. I'm looking for a capstone, and I can't think of a better capstone to an academic career than the flagship university of the state of Alabama."
—Dr. Robert Witt, on being named President of UA in 2003

What was the name of Alexandra Robbins' 2004 book in which the author went undercover as a sorority member at several universities, including UA?

Pledged: The Secret Life of Sororities.

What UA program, conceived of in 1972 and launched in 1975, was the first in the Southeast?

UA's Department of Women's Studies. The program began offering MA degrees in 1988.

What UA institution, which celebrates its 100th anniversary in 2005, has a name that is based on one of their products? Where was it originally located?

The SUPe Store—The University of Alabama's Supply Store had a lunch counter and served soup. The name evolved from there. In the Union building, now known as Reese-Phifer Hall.

Which two very different world-famous New York dance companies conduct summer workshops on the UA campus?

The American Ballet Theatre and the Radio City Music Hall Rockettes. The American Ballet Theatre's workshop at UA is the only one held outside of New York or in partnership with a university.

Which fictional Alabama lawyer lends his name to the UA Law Library online catalog?

The catalog is named ATTICUS after Atticus Finch, the hero of *To Kill a Mockingbird* by UA graduate Harper Lee.

Before being known as the College of Human Environmental Science, what was the college called?

The School of Home Economics.

What unlikely department was once under the umbrella of Home Economics?

The art department.

Sports

What former UA basketball star was known nationally for his red shoes, or "crimson slippers"?

Antoine Pettway.

Who is credited as giving Paul "Bear" Bryant his first houndstooth hat, which remains an icon to this day? By what moniker is he best known?

Mel Allen, UA alum (1932 and 1936) and lifelong friend of Coach Bryant. As "the voice of the New York Yankees."

Where did Allen and Bryant meet?

They both were students at The University of Alabama in the 1930s.

"Crimson and white are simply the most beautiful colors I have ever seen."

—An anony-mous UA fan

What baseball hall of famer began the 1920 season at UA as team captain?

Joe Sewell.

What future U.S. president entertained the 1938 UA Rose Bowl team on their visit to Hollywood?

Ronald Reagan.

What is the CAVE?

The Coleman Auxiliary Volleyball Extension—an expansion of Coleman Coliseum that opened in 1996 and houses the UA volleyball team.

Name the former UA defensive tackle turned entrepreneur who ate 43 slices of pizza to raise money to fight cystic fibrosis.

Bob Baumhower, whose name in Tuscaloosa brings to mind both football and Wings!

What year was the first UA Annual Cheerleader Reunion held?

In 1976, after the Alabama vs. Southern Mississippi game.

What well-known British comedian visited Tuscaloosa in 2002 and filmed a bit for his HBO hit comedy in Bryant-Denny Stadium?

Sasha Baron Cohen, or as he's best known, Ali G. He appeared as his Austrian TV reporter character, Bruno.

What UA football star did he interview?

Shaud Williams, who was an incredibly gracious interviewee.

What year was the first University of Alabama football team formed? Who did UA play? What was the final score?

1892. Birmingham High School. 56-0.

What UA football legend appeared as himself on
The Simpsons **and** ***The Brady Bunch*,** **proving both**
lasting power and his place as an American icon.

Former UA quarterback Joe Namath—both his face
and his name are as recognizable today as they were
when he played with the Tide in the 1960s.

How many national championships in football
has the Crimson Tide won? Name the years.

Twelve—in 1925, 1926, 1930, 1934, 1941, 1961,
1964, 1965, (and any fan will agree it should have
been 1966, too!), 1973, 1978, 1979 and 1992—
the most championships by any SEC team and
among the most of any school in the country.

How many of those national championships were won
by Coach Paul "Bear" Bryant.

Coach Bryant led Alabama to six national championships—the most of any coach.

Who was the youngest head coach of the Crimson Tide
football program?

Wallace Wade, who was hired in 1923 at the age of 31.

Who was the youngest football coach hired in Alabama's modern era?

Mike Shula. Alabama's 26th head coach was 38 years old when hired in 2003.

How many times did the Crimson Tide play in the Rose Bowl? How many were losses? What was UA's biggest Rose Bowl victory? What year? Who did they play?

Six times. One—The Tide won four out of six and tied one. The score was 24-0. 1931. Washington State.

What two Sugar Bowl records does the Crimson Tide hold?

It is the only team to have won three consecutive Sugar Bowl championships (1978, 1979 and 1980), and with eight victories, UA holds the Sugar Bowl record for most wins.

How many University of Alabama players have been inducted into the National College Football Hall of Fame?

Eight.

How did "The Crimson Tide" get its name? What game was he describing when using that term?

It's purported to have been started by Hugh Roberts, a former sports editor of the *Birmingham Age-Herald.* An Alabama-Auburn game played in Birmingham in 1907.

What was he referring to?

A rain-soaked field and Alabama's valiant efforts to hold the heavily favored Auburn team to a 6-6 tie.

What sports writer is credited for popularizing the name in the media?

Zipp Newman used the name often—he was a former sports editor of the *Birmingham News.*

What were popular nicknames before then?

"The Thin Red Line," and the "Crimson-White."

What year did 'Bama renew football relations with their archrival Auburn?

1948—They hadn't played each other for forty-one years.

Was the forty-one-year gap just in football?

No—the schools did not compete with each other in football, basketball, track and baseball, with the exception of two post-season tournaments.

In what years were those two basketball tournaments?

1924 and 1941.

What 1935 Rose Bowl MVP went on to play professional baseball with the Cincinnati Reds?

Dixie Howell.

Who coached the "rocket eight"?

Johnny Dee.

What 1950s UA basketball player held sixteen (of eighteen) UA individual records?

Jerry Harper.

What UA grad has scored over 15,000 professional career points, and has been named to the NBA All-Star team four times?

Latrell Sprewell (class of 1992).

What two former UA students played against each other in the 1932 World Series, sharing the field with Babe Ruth and Lou Gehrig?

Joe Sewell, who played for the New York Yankees, and Riggs Stephenson of the Chicago Cubs. The Yankees won.

What member of the 1933 football team was named for a Wild West performer, a man who was also his godfather?

B'Ho Kirkland—a lineman for the Tide. B'Ho means "Brother of the Crippled One."

What was the "Baby Tide"?

The UA freshman squad.

> "I love the University. I have given my life to it. Some day I hope to write its history. I am a fatalist enough, and old enough to be resigned to my fate whatever it may be. But I hope that I shall never be so old, or so fatalist that I will not fight for any battle affecting the University. I will not stand on the sidelines but will enter the fight, and enjoy it."
> **—President George H. Denny at the alumni banquet, 1935**

What UA Coach, inducted into the Alabama Sports Hall of Fame in 2003, is the only inductee in a particular sport?

Coach Sarah Patterson, UA's head gymnastics coach.

What current NBA player and UA alum has more NBA championships under his belt than any other active player?

Robert Horry (class of 1992), with five NBA championships.

What NBA record did he break during the NBA Finals in 2005?

Most three-pointers made by any player in the NBA Finals, surpassing Michael Jordan's record of 42 three-point shots.

Who played Paul "Bear" Bryant in the 1984 film *The Bear*?

Gary Busey, who also played Buddy Holly in *The Buddy Holly Story.*

Who was "The Dothan Antelope"?

Johnny Mack Brown.

Besides being a UA Rose Bowl MVP, what was Johnny Mack Brown known for?

A prolific star of Westerns, he made movies in Hollywood, signing with MGM in 1926 and appearing in his last film in 1966.

Which UA athlete set an NCAA, American and international record in 1977?

Casey Converse, who set all three records for the 1,650 Freestyle event. He was the first swimmer in history to go under 15 minutes in the mile.

Name two other "cowboys" that once played for the Crimson Tide.

Lee Roy Jordan went on to play for the Dallas Cowboys from 1963 to 1976, was their all-time tackle leader and is in the Cowboys Ring of Honor. Dennis Homan played with the Cowboys from 1968 to 1970,

What annual reunion started in 1996, showing just how important Coach Bryant is to UA fans?

The annual Paul "Bear" Bryant Namesake Reunion, held at the Bryant Museum every fall since 1996. Conceived of by Paul Bryant Jr., more than 600 namesakes have been recorded to date.

What was the last game that Coach Bryant coached? Who did Alabama play? What was the score of that game? Who was the MVP of that game?

The 1982 Liberty Bowl. Illinois. Alabama beat Illinois 21-15. Jeremiah Castille.

How many games did Coach Bryant win in his career?

A record 323 games.

How many times was Coach Bryant voted National Coach of the Year?

Three times. The award is now named in his honor!

What UA quarterback led Alabama to its first victory over the Fighting Irish?

Mike Shula—in a 1986 Kickoff Classic, Alabama defeated Notre Dame 28-10.

What distinction does the first captain of the Auburn football team have?

Frank Lupton, Auburn's first captain in 1892, was the first person to be born in the UA President's Mansion— he was the son of UA President Nathanial Lupton.

What former UA basketball star stepped into the shoes of one of the most controversial college basketball coaches of all time? How did he stand out at Alabama?

Mike Davis, who replaced Bobby Knigh at Indiana University in 2001. Davis was the first coach in Indiana history to begin his tenure with three straight 20-plus win seasons and three straight NCAA Tournament appearances and is Indiana's first African American head coach. He played for the Tide from 1979-83.

Give the surname of the family who had seven sons, five of whom made letters as pitchers for Crimson Tide baseball. What else were they known for?

Lary—The Lary Brothers, Joe, Al, Ed, Frank and Gene all pitched for the Tide, three of them going on to play professionally. The two other brothers were great pitchers too, but WWII prevented them from attending UA. Fiddling—They were all musicians. Al and Ed also played football at Alabama.

Name the one person who was a member of the coaching staff for all six modern era national championships.

Current Athletic Director Mal Moore, who was Coach Bryant's graduate assistant in 1964, Alabama's defensive backfield coach in 1965 and offensive coordinator for the 1973, 1978, 1979 and 1992 national championships.

How did Mal Moore get his start with the Crimson Tide?

As a player—he completed his undergraduate degree from UA in 1963, a master's degree in 1964 and played football under Coach Bryant.

For what game did the Tide football team first wear crimson helmets? What color had they been previously? In what year did the team first start wearing hard football helmets?

> The 1960 Astro-Bluebonnet Bowl against Texas. White with crimson stripes. 1930.

What former UA student won a bronze medal in the 1972 Olympics in Munich?

> Jan Johnson, in the pole vault.

How many national championships in women's gymnastics has UA won? In what years?

> Four. 1988, 1991, 1996 and 2002.

How many UA gymnasts have been named SEC Athletes of the Year, an honor that spans all sports?

> Four—Penny Hauschild in 1985, Dee Foster in 1990, Andree Pickens in 2002, and Jeana Rice in 2004.

"The University can be many things for many people, but for the serious student it was and is the citadel and garden of mind."

—E.O. Wilson, UA alum

Which two common household cleaning items are often fastened together to create signs at Alabama football games?

A box of Tide detergent and two rolls of toilet paper (roll, Tide, roll).

Under what coach did Paul "Bear" Bryant play football at Alabama?

Coach Frank Thomas.

Who is credited for bringing football to The University of Alabama? In what year?

W.G. Little of Livingston Alabama. 1892.

What game brought Alabama football its first real national recognition? What was the score of that game?

The 1922 game where the Tide traveled to Philadelphia and defeated the powerful University of Pennsylvania team. Alabama beat Penn 9-7.

When was Alabama's first undefeated and untied football season?

The 1925 season was the first, under Coach Wallace Wade.

How many undefeated teams did coach Frank Thomas coach? Who was his college roommate?

Three—1934, 1936 and 1945. "The Gipper"—Football legend George Gipp. They were roommates at Notre Dame.

What former UA assistant coach passed away just one hour before his induction into the Alabama Sports Hall of Fame? Under how many coaches did he serve at UA?

Hank Crisp. Five head coaches—he was at UA for 36 years, serving as AD twice during that tenure.

What remarkable piece of early Super Bowl history gives Alabama fans even more pride in the Tide?

The first three Super Bowl MVPs were Alabama alums—Bart Starr won it in January 1967 and 1968 for the 1966 and 1967 football seasons, and Joe Namath took the MVP in January 1969 for the 1968 season.

What building on campus was once known as the "Plaid Palace"? Why? Who is it named for? When was it built? What was it originally called?

Coleman Coliseum. In honor of former UA basketball coach Wimp Sanderson. Sanderson had a penchant for loud plaid sport coats. It was named for Jeff Coleman, a UA alum and administrator who never missed a UA bowl game. 1968. Memorial Coliseum.

Have football seasons ever been cancelled at Alabama?

Yes—in 1892, part of 1897 and 1898, when a faculty ruling prohibited games off-campus, and again in 1918 and 1943 because of war.

How did the UA team travel to the 1935 Rose Bowl?

In a special train—it traveled across the country, leaving Tuscaloosa on December 21 for the January 5 game.

What former UA athlete won a medal in the 2004 Olympics in Athens?

Susan (Bartholomew) Williams won the bronze in Triathlon.

What UA alum won four gold medals at two consecutive Olympics?

Swimmer Jon Olsen—in the 400m and 800m free relays in the 1996 games in Atlanta, where he was also the team captain, and in the 400m free relay and 400m medley relay in Barcelona—along with a bronze in the 800m free relay.

Who are the Crimson Cabaret?

UA's dance team—a favorite at Tide basketball games!

Who was Everett Strupper?

A sports writer for the *Atlanta Journal-Constitution*, after hearing fans in the stands yelling, "Here come the elephants," Alabama's massive linemen. He described them on October 8, 1930, in his paper as "Red Elephants." The name stuck.

What was Alabama's overall record that year?

10-0.

How many shutouts did UA have that year? How many points did Alabama score that season? What was the crowning achievement for that season?

A remarkable eight—allowing only 13 points to be scored on them all season. 217. A 24-0 victory at the Rose Bowl and being named national champions.

Name the UA athlete that took a first place for the 2004-05 year in a track and field event.

Beth Mallory, who won first place in the discus, winning by more than seven feet. Her win marked the first UA track and field national championship since 1989.

What UA alum, competing for the Bahamas, won two medals in the 2000 Summer Olympics in Sydney?

Runner Pauline Davis took a gold in the 4x100 meter relay and a silver in the 200 meter dash.

Who was the first African-American men's scholarship basketball player at UA?

Wendell Thomas Hudson, who came to UA in 1970.

What UA alum won a gold in the 1984 Los Angeles Olympics and a silver in Seoul in 1988?

Runner Lillie Leatherwood, in the 4x400 meter relay.

What former UA basketball star made history as the first basketball Olympian at Alabama?

Antonio McDyess—he won a gold medal in the 2000 Olympics in Sydney.

Name the former UA baseball star who in that same year brought home a gold medal for baseball.

Tim Young.

What former UA head football coach was one of Coach Bryant's "Junction Boys"? What coaching victory did he have against his mentor?

Gene Stallings. As coach of Texas A&M, Stallings's team beat Alabama in the Cotton Bowl in 1967.

What NFL team did Gene Stallings coach?

The St. Louis Cardinals.

What member of the 1961 championship football team went on to coach at Tide archrival Tennessee?

Bill Battle.

Under what coach did 'Bama baseball achieve six SEC championships?

Coach Tilden "Happy" Campbell had a lot to be happy about, achieving SEC championships in six of his first eight seasons at UA.

In what year did UA's baseball team pitch a perfect game?

In 1993—Al Drumheller, John Collins and Brett Sullenberger pitched it in six innings at South Florida on March 31 of that year.

What UA All-American football player and humanitarian became in 2002 the first African-American general manager in NFL history?

Ozzie Newsome Jr.

What UA alum once held the Major League record for most consecutive baseball games played?

Joe Sewell—for 1,103 games. The record was bested by Lou Gehrig en route to his celebrated streak of 2,130 straight games.

What are the unofficial snack and drink of the Crimson Tide fan?

Golden Flake potato chips and Coca-Cola—they were the sponsors of *The Bear Bryant Show*, his Sunday post-game TV show.

Name the father of a former UA player who served as the chaplain for UA athletes for many years.

The Reverend Sylvester Croom Sr. He later served as a Tuscaloosa pastor and community leader.